LIFE IN THE UNITED KINGDOM

Home Office

Published by TSO (The Stationery Office) and
available from:

Online
www.tsoshop.co.uk

Mail, Telephone, Fax & E-mail
TSO
PO Box 29, Norwich NR3 1GN
Telephone orders/General enquiries: 0870
6005522
Fax orders: 0870 6005533
E-mail: customer.services@tso.co.uk
Textphone: 0870 240 3701

TSO Shops
16 Arthur Street, Belfast BT1 4GD
028 9023 8451
Fax 028 9023 5401
71 Lothian Road, Edinburgh EH3 9AZ
0870 606 5566
Fax 0870 606 5588

TSO@Blackwell and other Accredited Agents

First published 2008

Second Impression 2008

ISBN 978-0-11-341324-9

Printed in UK for The Stationery Office

N5935798 c100 10/08

CONTENTS

Acknowledgements   iv

Photographic credits   iv

Preface   v

Explanation of symbols   vi

A note about the structure of this guide   vii

Chapter 1: ABOUT THE LIFE IN THE UK TEST   1

Chapter 2: A CHANGING SOCIETY   21

Chapter 3: UK TODAY: A PROFILE   35

Chapter 4: HOW THE UK IS GOVERNED   49

Chapter 5: EVERYDAY NEEDS   63

Chapter 6: EMPLOYMENT   77

Appendix: A TEST TO ASSESS YOUR READING LEVEL   91

ADDITIONAL SOURCES OF INFORMATION   101

Acknowledgements

The publisher would like to acknowledge the following individuals and organisations for their contribution to this study guide:

- Deborah Kahn from Publishing Directions

- The National Institute of Adult Continuing Education (NIACE)

- The Advisory Board on Naturalisation and Integration (ABNI)

Photographic credits

Pages v and 48
i-stock

Pages 2 and 11
TSO

Pages 5 and 80
PhotoDisc

Pages viii, 8, 10, 12, 13, 16, 22, 34, 36, 50, 51, 58, 62, 64, 66, 74, 78, 93, 94, 95, 102
Dreamstime

Page 15
www.lifeintheuktest.gov.uk

Page 18
Brent Council

Page 20
Imran Hayat-Khan

Page 92
ComStock

Congratulations!

You have decided that you would like to live in the UK permanently or to apply to become a British citizen. You will probably be planning to take the Life in the UK Test as the next step in your application process. You might be wondering how to apply and what the test will involve.

The Life in the UK Test is based on the content of the Home Office publication, *Life in the United Kingdom: A Journey to Citizenship*, published by The Stationery Office (TSO), so you will need to make sure that you have a copy and that you read it carefully. The book that you are reading now is a study guide which can be used together with the main Home Office publication, and tells you everything you need to know about taking the Life in the UK Test. It also contains some sample questions which are like the questions which you will get on the day. These are **not** the actual questions which you will take in the test, but you can use them to find out whether you are ready to take the test.

Good luck with your studying and with taking the test!

Explanation of symbols

Warning

Take heed of the information which accompanies this symbol. It could save you making a mistake, and make your application progress more smoothly.

Important information

It is vital that you read this. It contains information that you need to know when applying for UK citizenship.

Tip

Follow this advice, and you could save yourself a lot of time and trouble.

A note about the structure of this guide

 Note that this study guide is **not** a replacement for the main publication, *Life in the UK: A Journey to Citizenship*. You will need to read the main book in order to prepare thoroughly for the test.

Before you start, it is worth understanding how this study guide is structured.

Chapter 1 provides you with general information about the Life in the UK Test, who needs to take it and what you need to do to prepare for it. You will learn what the test consists of, how to apply for it, and what to expect on the day of the test. It will also tell you what happens after the test, depending on whether or not you have passed.

Chapters 2 to 6 consist mainly of practice questions. Each chapter has the same number as the relevant chapter in the main publication, *Life in the UK: A Journey to Citizenship*. For example, Chapter 2 in the study guide will test your knowledge of Chapter 2 in the main book; Chapter 3 will test you on Chapter 3 in the main book, and so on. Each chapter contains 40 practice questions, and answers and helpful pointers are given at the end of each chapter. You will only be tested on the information contained within Chapters 2 to 6 in the main book – hence the study guide questions end on Chapter 6. However, you might find it easier to answer some of the test questions if you have read Chapter 1 in the main book, which gives a lot of background information about the UK.

Although there are no test questions on Chapters 7 to 9 of the main book, you will find lots of useful information in them. Chapter 9 will help you if you want to get to know people in your local community. If you want to go on to apply for UK citizenship in the future, you might be able to do this more quickly if you have done some voluntary work. Chapter 9 gives you some good ideas about this.

Chapter 1
ABOUT THE LIFE IN THE UK TEST

Summary of the chapter content

This chapter contains essential information about the test, including:

- what the test is

- who has to take it

- what to do if your English is not good enough

- how to prepare for the test

- how to book the test

- what types of question appear in the test

- what happens on the day of the test

- what happens after the test

- what to expect if you get invited to a citizenship ceremony

INTRODUCTION

Background

If you are reading this book, it is probably because you have taken the very important decision to apply to live in the United Kingdom permanently or to become a British citizen. Taking either of these decisions is an incredibly important step in your life. To prepare for living in this country permanently and for making a long-term commitment to the UK, there are things about the language, history and culture of the UK that you will need to know. That is why the Life in the UK Test was introduced in November 2005. Studying for the test gives you the practical knowledge that you need to live in this country and to take part in society.

What is the Life in the UK Test?

If you want to apply to be a British citizen or for permanent residence in the UK (also called 'settlement' or 'indefinite leave to remain'), you will have to show that you have reached a certain level of ability in understanding the English language and in your knowledge about life in the UK. There are two ways of showing that you have reached this level. You can take an English for Speakers of Other Languages (ESOL) course, which uses teaching materials containing citizenship topics (more on this later), or you can take the Life in the UK Test.

The Life in the UK Test consists of 24 questions about aspects of life in Britain today. You take the test on a computer in an official test centre. You have 45 minutes to complete the test. The questions in the test are based on Chapters 2, 3, 4, 5 and 6 of the second edition of the book *Life in the United Kingdom: A Journey to Citizenship* published by The Stationery Office (TSO). These chapters cover the following topics:

- **How society in Britain is changing (Chapter 2)**: information about the history of immigration to the UK; the changing roles of women; and the lifestyle patterns of children, families and young people.

- **A profile of the UK today (Chapter 3):** information about the composition of the population of the UK; the nations and regions which make up the UK; the UK's religions and religious freedom; and the customs and traditions which are celebrated in the UK.

- **How the UK is governed (Chapter 4)**: information about Britain's system of government; and its relationship to Europe, the Commonwealth and the United Nations.

- **Everyday needs (Chapter 5)**: information about housing; services in and for the home; personal finance; health, education and leisure services; travel and transport; and the need for identity documents.

- **Employment (Chapter 6):** information about looking for a job; training and volunteering; your rights and responsibilities at work; and childcare and children in employment.

You must read *Life in the United Kingdom: A Journey to Citizenship* in order to pass the Life in the UK Test. Most people who fail the test have either not read this book, or do not yet have good enough English to take it. This study guide, the *Official Citizenship Test Study Guide*, is not a substitute for reading the book. It is a guide to help you to prepare for the test and will help you to know if you are ready for it.

In this study guide you will find information about how to apply for the test and about what to expect when taking the test. There is information about what is in the chapters you need to read in *Life in the United Kingdom: A Journey to Citizenship* and some examples of the types of question that you might be asked about each of those chapters when you take the test. These questions will help you to make sure that you have understood what is in the book. The study guide also gives some other tips about studying for the test. It is important to remember that each person will be given different questions in the test. The questions in this book are **not** the questions that you will get in the test.

You should know that other 'study guides' for the Life in the UK Test are not official, even though some may suggest that they are. This means that they may not provide the support you need. Some may even mislead you by suggesting that you memorise answers to questions that are not real and are very different from the ones you will be asked in your test.

Who has to take the test?

You will need to take the Life in the UK Test if you plan to apply for naturalisation as a British citizen or for indefinite leave to remain (settlement). The test is only suitable for you if your level of English is at ESOL Entry 3 or above. If your level of English is lower than ESOL Entry 3, then you will need to take the ESOL and citizenship classes (see below). You can assess whether your English is at ESOL Entry 3 by taking the test in the appendix at the back of this book, 'A Test to Assess Your Reading Level'.

You should take the Life in the UK Test before you apply for naturalisation as a British citizen or before you apply for indefinite leave to remain. Remember that you need to meet all the other requirements.

You do **not** need to take the test if you:

- are under 18 or aged 65 years or over

- have a long-term illness or disability that severely restricts mobility and ability to attend language classes

- have a learning difficulty that means you are unable to learn another language

Additionally, if you are applying for indefinite leave to remain, you may not have to take the test if you:

- qualify for permanent residence under the domestic violence rules

- are the citizen of another country on discharge from HM Forces (including Gurkhas where the qualifying period has been met) or are the husband, wife or civil partner of the citizen of another country on discharge from HM Forces (including Gurkhas).

- are a bereaved husband, wife, civil partner or unmarried partner of a person settled in the UK

- are applying for residence as a parent, grandparent or other dependent relative of a person settled in the UK

- are applying as a financially independent retired person

- are the husband, wife, civil partner, or unmarried or same-sex partner of a British citizen or of a permanent resident of the UK who is a permanent member of HM Diplomatic Service, a staff member of the British Council on a tour of duty abroad, or staff member of the Department for International Development

- are a citizen of the European Economic Area who is applying under the rules allowing free movement

- are a citizen of Turkey applying under the rules of the European Community Association Agreement with Turkey for establishing in business in the UK

- are applying on completion of a qualifying period of discretional leave, exceptional leave or humanitarian protection

These exceptions do not apply if you are applying for citizenship.

 You only have to pass the Life in the UK Test **once**. If you take and pass the Life in the UK Test as part of your application for permanent residence, you will not need to take another test if you apply for British citizenship later. You should keep your test pass certificate safe so that you can use it again.

What should I do if my English is not good enough?

If your reading level of English is lower than ESOL Entry 3 and you wish to apply for citizenship or indefinite leave to remain (settlement), you will need to attend ESOL and citizenship classes. ESOL and citizenship classes help you to improve your English and learn more about life in the UK. They are also a good way of meeting new people. You can take these classes at your local further education or community college. To find out more about ESOL and citizenship classes, contact your local college, or call the Life in the UK Test helpline on 0800 0154245.

 If your level of English is below ESOL Entry 3, then you will only have to pass an ESOL exam in speaking and listening. You will **not** have to take the Life in the UK Test.

 Some private colleges are now offering short ESOL courses that are very expensive and do not really make your English any better. If you want to study at a private college, you should make sure it has 'English UK' accreditation, otherwise you risk wasting your money.

 You can assess whether your reading level in English is at ESOL Entry 3 by completing the test in the appendix at the back of this book (A Test to Assess Your Reading Level).

Is the test only available in English?

The Life in the UK Test is offered in English. However, if you are taking the test in a centre in Wales, you may ask to take the test in the Welsh language, or if you are taking the test in Scotland, you may ask to take the test in Scottish Gaelic. Special arrangements have to be made for this. You can get further details from your test centre.

Where can I find out more information about the test?

If you still have questions after reading through this book and *Life in the United Kingdom: A Journey to Citizenship*, you can contact the Life in the UK Test helpline on 0800 0154245 or go to the website http://www.lifeintheuktest.gov.uk/ for more information.

PREPARING FOR THE TEST

Studying for the test

To pass the Life in the UK Test, you need to know the contents of Chapters 2, 3, 4, 5 and 6 of the book *Life in the United Kingdom: A Journey to Citizenship* very well. There is a lot of information contained in the book, so it is a good idea to think about how you are going to prepare for the test. Everyone learns in different ways. We suggest a number of techniques below which might help you to understand and remember the content of *Life in the United Kingdom: A Journey to Citizenship*.

When to study

- Plan in advance when you are going to study – make yourself a timetable and give yourself enough time before your test date to learn the information you need to know. Make sure you have a quiet place where you can study.

- Study for short periods and have a break regularly. If you get tired, it will be hard to concentrate.

  If you need a quiet place to study, the local library may be a good place if there is nowhere quiet where you live.

CHECK YOUR UNDERSTANDING

- After reading each section, ask yourself 'What was the main point?' If you can describe it to yourself in your own words, then you have understood and you are more likely to remember it and to be able to answer questions about it.

MAKE NOTES

- Have a pencil or pen and some small pieces of paper available.

- After reading each section, decide what the main points are and write the important facts onto the pieces of paper. Do not write too much as they need to be easy to scan.

PRACTICE QUESTIONS

- When you have finished each chapter, complete the practice questions in this book. If you find that you have got something wrong, the answers section will point you to the section of *Life in the United Kingdom: A Journey to Citizenship* which you need to go back to and read again.

REVISION

- Whenever you have a spare moment, read through some of your index cards or pieces of paper with your notes on, or stick them on the wall somewhere in your home and look at them regularly. Reviewing your notes often will help you to remember the information on them.

- It might help to study together with a friend who is also taking the test. You can discuss parts of the book that were difficult to understand and test each other's knowledge.

- English-speaking friends, neighbours or people at work might be able to help you. This is also a good way to get to know people better, because even British people don't know all the answers!

 If you find revision difficult, ask a friend or family member to test you on information on your index cards or directly from the book.

Making sure that your computer skills are good enough to take the test

You have to take the test on a computer at an official test centre. If you have never used a computer or do not use a computer often, then it would be a good idea to improve your computer skills before going to take your test.

You could go to your local Learndirect centre. You can find them in local sports clubs, leisure and community centres, churches, libraries, on university campuses and even in some railway stations. They will provide you with access to a computer, free internet access and a range of courses to get you started. To find your nearest Learndirect centre, you can call free on 0800 101 901.

If you live in England, there is a lot of help available at your local UK online centre. These are centres which try to provide everyone with access to computers near their home. There are 6,000 UK online centres and they can be found on high streets and in libraries, internet cafés and community centres. They have staff and volunteers ready to give you help and advice on how to get started with using a computer. To find out the address and phone number of your nearest centre, you can call free on 0800 77 1234.

If you live in Scotland, Wales or Northern Ireland, most local libraries offer free or low-cost computer and internet access.

Once you have started to use a computer, you might want to go to the Life in the UK Test website (http://www.lifeintheuktest.gov.uk) where you will find training on how to use the mouse and keyboard in the section 'Prepare for the test'. You should also visit the navigation tutorial in the same section to learn how to find your way around the test. You can do the tutorial as many times as you want – it will help you to feel comfortable about answering questions on the computer.

Practise taking the test

Before you take the test you should complete the practice questions in this book. In addition, there are practice questions on the Life in the UK Test website (http://www.lifeintheuktest.gov.uk) in the section 'Prepare for the test: what you need to know'.

When you go to the test centre to take the Life in the UK Test, you can do a practice test of four questions before you start the proper test. You will have four minutes to do this practice test and you are allowed to take it twice.

TAKING THE TEST

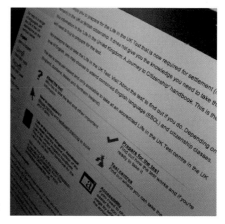

Booking the test

WHERE CAN I TAKE THE TEST?

There are 100 Life in the UK test centres around the country where you can take the test. Most of them are also learning centres where you can improve your language or computer skills if you need to. You can find out where your nearest test centres are by going to the 'Find a test centre' section of the website http://www.lifeintheuktest.gov.uk. If you type in your post code, it will show you the contact details for the five nearest test centres to where you live. Alternatively, you can call the Life in the UK Test helpline on 0800 0154245.

HOW DO I BOOK A TEST?

You can book a test by visiting or telephoning your local test centre.

HOW LONG WILL I HAVE TO WAIT BEFORE I TAKE THE TEST?

The test centre will offer you a place in one of their test sessions within one to four weeks of your request. You will have to wait at least seven days between making your booking and being able to take the test.

HOW MUCH WILL THE TEST COST AND HOW DO I PAY FOR IT?

The test costs £34 (as of August 2008). You must pay this fee at your test centre before you take the test. You can pay the fee in cash. Some of the test centres also accept credit or debit cards. Payment details will be given to you by the test centre when you contact them to make the booking.

 If you do not pay the test fee, you will not be allowed to take the test and will have to pay a £10 late cancellation fee.

WHAT IF I NEED TO CANCEL OR CHANGE THE TEST DATE?

If you have to change the day of your test, you must tell your test centre. If you give less than seven days' notice, the test centre may charge a £10 late cancellation fee. Please check with the test centre about their rules before you book your test.

WHAT DO I NEED TO BRING WITH ME?

You **must** bring photographic identification (ID) with you to the test centre to show to the test supervisor. You will **not** be allowed to take the test without your photographic ID.

Please make sure that the photos on the documents do look like you or they may not be accepted.

You must bring one of the following forms of ID:

- a passport from your country of origin

- a UK photocard driving licence, full or provisional

- one of the following Home Office travel documents:

    - a Convention Travel Document (CTD)
    - a Certificate of Identity Document (CID), or
    - a Stateless Person Document (SPD)

- an Immigration Status Document, endorsed with a UK Residence Permit and bearing a photo of the holder (which must be together on the same document)

If you have had any letters from the Home Office, you will have a Home Office reference number. Please take this to the test centre with you on the day you take your test. Please also take proof of your postcode: this could be a bank statement, utility bill or letter from the Home Office.

I AM DISABLED. WILL THE TEST CENTRE BE ABLE TO HELP ME?

Yes. Tell your test supervisor about any special needs when you book your test. This will allow the test centre to make any arrangements to give you the support you need. This will make sure that your disability does not affect your test result. You may also be able to have a longer test time of 90 minutes if you need it.

Taking the test

WHAT DOES THE TEST CONSIST OF?

The test consists of 24 questions which are based on information that can be found in Chapters 2, 3, 4, 5 and 6 of *Life in the United Kingdom: A Journey to Citizenship*.

 The questions only cover information in Chapters 2, 3, 4, 5 and 6 of the *Life in the United Kingdom: A Journey to Citizenship* and not from anywhere else.

Each participant has to answer 24 different questions which are chosen by a computer.

There are four types of question in the test.

The first type of question involves selecting one correct answer from four options. Here is an example of this type of question.

Where is the Prime Minister's official home in London?

- ☐ Downing Street
- ☐ Parliament Square
- ☐ Richmond Terrace
- ☐ Whitehall Place

(The correct answer is Downing Street.)

The second type of question involves deciding whether a statement is true or false. Here is an example of this second type of question.

Is the statement below TRUE or FALSE?

Citizens of the UK can vote in elections at the age of 18.

☐　TRUE
☐　FALSE

(The correct answer is TRUE.)

The third type of question involves selecting the statement which you think is correct from a choice of two statements. Here is an example of this third type of question.

Which of these statements is correct?

☐　Scottish bank notes are valid in all parts of the UK.
☐　Scottish bank notes are valid only in Scotland.

(The first statement is the correct answer.)

The final type of question involves selecting two correct answers from four options. You need to select **both** correct answers to get a point on this type of question. Here is an example of this fourth type of question.

Which TWO places can you go to if you need a National Insurance number?

☐　Department for Education and Skills
☐　Home Office
☐　Jobcentre Plus
☐　Social security office

(The correct answers are Jobcentre Plus and social security office.)

HOW DO I TAKE THE TEST?

You take the test using a computer. You will have 45 minutes to do the test. This gives you plenty of time to choose your answers and check them again before the end. You do not need to rush to finish the test quickly; remember to use all of the time that you are given. Headphones are available for you to listen to the questions and answer options.

Figure 1 gives you an idea of what format the test will take. It is worth taking time to familiarise yourself with the layout.

You can move quickly to any question in the test by simply selecting a box with your mouse or keyboard.

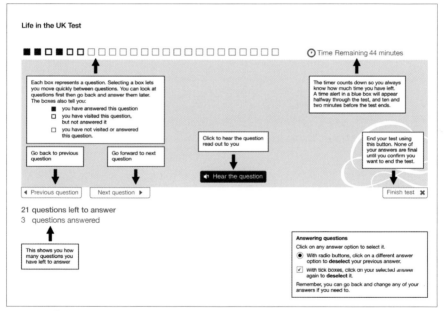

Figure 1 Life in the UK Test – navigation tutorial

WHAT IS THE PASS MARK?

The pass mark is 75%, so you have to get 18 questions right to pass.

What happens on the day of the test?

REGISTRATION

The test centre will tell you what time to arrive at the centre.

 Please do not arrive at the test centre with any children or friends as there may not be anywhere for them to wait. They cannot go into the test room with you.

You will pay for your test and your ID will be checked. Your personal details will be registered onto the test system and you will be asked to check that they are correct. Please check carefully, because after you click on the 'I agree' button, these details cannot be changed. It is your responsibility to check that they are correct.

When entering your personal details onto the test system, be careful about your spelling. The details must be the same as the ones on your documents. You will be asked to sign a list stating the day you did the test.

TEST SESSION

When registration is complete for all the candidates taking the test with you, the test supervisor will explain the test process and test conditions. At this point you can ask any questions that you might have.

The test supervisor will authorise access to the test system for you. You will be asked to confirm your details (name, date of birth and nationality) on the screen. Do this carefully to make sure you get the right test!

You can take a practice test so that you can practise answering questions with the mouse and moving from one question to another. This practice test does not affect your final result in the real test. You can take the practice test twice. The practice test allows you to relax before taking the real test.

You will **not** be allowed to look at books or any notes you have made during the test. You will not be able to use any electronic device such as a mobile phone, bluetooth headphones, blackberry or palm pilot. If you are caught cheating, your test will be stopped immediately. You will not get your money back and you will be reported to the Home Office. This will have a negative effect on your application.

When you finish the test, leave the room quietly. You will receive your result at the end of the test session. It will either be a Pass Notification Letter or a Results Notification Letter (Fail) (see section below).

AFTER THE TEST

If you pass the test

If you pass the test, the test supervisor will give you a Pass Notification Letter. Both you and the test supervisor must sign this letter. The letter contains details of your test date, supervisor, centre location and a unique ID number.

You will need the Pass Notification Letter when you apply for settlement or citizenship, so it is very important to keep it safe. It is not possible to get another copy of the Pass Notification Letter, so if you lose it, you will need to take the test again.

When you have completed your application for citizenship or indefinite leave to remain, you need to attach your Pass Notification Letter and send both to the Home Office. The Home Office will keep the information it gets from test centres for a reasonable period of time. However, you should send in your application as soon as possible after taking the test.

If you do not pass the test

Your test supervisor will tell you if you have failed the test and will give you a Results Notification Letter. In this case you will need to take the test again. You will need to book and pay for another appointment and you will have to wait for at least seven days before you can retake the test. You can take the test as many times as you need to. You cannot make an application for naturalisation as a British citizen or for indefinite leave to remain until you have passed the test.

Before you retake the test, it would be a good idea to read *Life in the United Kingdom: A Journey to Citizenship* again and do the exercises in 'Prepare for the test' on http://www.lifeintheuktest.gov.uk until you feel confident. Your Results Notification Letter will tell you which questions you got wrong, as well as give feedback on which areas of the handbook you need to look at again.

If you feel you did not pass the test because of your level of English, you may want to think about going to combined English language (ESOL) and citizenship classes at your local further education college or adult education centre. If you do a course and get a certificate, you do **not** have to take the test again.

The citizenship ceremony

If your application for citizenship is successful, the Home Office will send you a letter confirming this and inviting you to attend a ceremony. Your ceremony will usually be close to where you live. If you want your ceremony to be somewhere else in the UK, you need to make this clear when you make your application for naturalisation.

When you receive your invitation to a ceremony, you have 90 days to attend one. Your invitation will include contact details for the local authority or council that will organise your ceremony. The ceremony usually takes place at a register office, but increasingly in another public/community building. Most local authorities arrange group ceremonies for everyone in the local area who is becoming a British citizen at that time. You will usually be able to take two guests with you to the ceremony. Attendance at the ceremony is by invitation only.

Alternatively, you can arrange a private ceremony. You should discuss your requirements with your local authority. You may have to pay an extra fee to arrange a private ceremony.

When you attend your ceremony, you must make an oath of allegiance (or you can make an affirmation if you prefer not to swear by God) and a pledge. These are the promises you make when you become a British citizen. The words of the oath, affirmation and pledge are all given below.

 You may wish to practise saying the oath or affirmation, and the pledge, before you attend the ceremony.

OATH OF ALLEGIANCE

I [name] swear by Almighty God that on becoming a British citizen, I will be faithful and bear true allegiance to Her Majesty Queen Elizabeth the Second, her Heirs and Successors, according to law.

AFFIRMATION OF ALLEGIANCE

I [name] do solemnly, sincerely and truly declare and affirm that on becoming a British citizen, I will be faithful and bear true allegiance to Her Majesty Queen Elizabeth the Second, her Heirs and Successors, according to law.

PLEDGE

I will give my loyalty to the United Kingdom and respect its rights and freedoms. I will uphold its democratic values. I will observe its laws faithfully and fulfil my duties and obligations as a British citizen.

Ceremonies in Wales

If you are attending a ceremony in Wales you may, if you wish, make the oath or affirmation, and the pledge, in Welsh. The Welsh version of the oath, affirmation and pledge are below.

LLW TEYRNGARWCH

Yr wyf i [enw], yn tyngu i Dduw Hollalluog y byddaf i, ar ôl dod yn ddinesydd Prydeinig, yn ffyddlon ac yn wir deyrngar i'w Mawrhydi y Frenhines Elisabeth yr Ail, ei Hetifeddion a'i Holynwyr, yn unol âr gyfraith.

CADARNHAU TEYRNGARWCH

Yr wyf i [enw], yn datgan ac yn cadarnhau yn ddifrifol, yn ddiffuant ac yn gywir y byddaf i, ar ôl dod yn ddinesydd Prydeinig, yn ffyddlon ac yn wir deyrngar i'w Mawrhydi y Frenhines Elisabeth yr Ail, ei Hetifeddion a'i Holynwyr, yn Unol âr gyfraith.

ADDUNED

Rhoddaf fy nheyrngarwch i'r Deyrnas Unedig ac fe barchaf ei hawliau a'i rhyddidau. Arddelaf ei gwerthoedd democrataidd. Glynaf yn ffyddlon wrth ei chyfreithiau a chyflawnaf fy nyletswyddau a'm rhwymedigaethau fel dinesydd Prydeinig.

Attending the ceremony

When you arrive at the ceremony, the staff will check your identity and confirm that the personal details on your certificate are correct.

During the ceremony, speeches will be made, often by important local or national people. These may include welcoming the new citizens on behalf of the local area and encouraging them to play an active role within their communities.

You will be presented with your certificate of British citizenship and a welcome pack. Sometimes, new citizens receive a small gift from the council. All new citizens are invited to stand while the national anthem is played.

Some local authorities arrange for photographs or videos of the event to be taken. You will be able to buy these if you would like to.

Chapter 2:
A CHANGING SOCIETY

This chapter provides a summary of the content of Chapter 2 of *Life in the United Kingdom: A Journey to Citizenship* and a set of test questions which will help you to examine your understanding of the chapter.

Summary of the chapter content

Migration to Britain

- The history of immigration to Britain; the reasons that people have come to Britain; the countries that they came from; the types of work that they came to do; and the changing government policies on immigration.

The changing role of women

- The changes to family structures and women's rights since the 19th century; the changing attitudes to women; and discrimination against women in the workplace and in education.

Children, family and young people

- Identity, interests, tastes and lifestyle patterns of children and young people; their education and work; health hazards; and their political and social attitudes.

Questions to test your understanding of
Chapter 2: A Changing Society

QUESTION 1   Is the statement below   ☐ TRUE or ☐ FALSE?

 'In the 1980s, the largest immigrant groups were from the West Indies, Ireland, India and Pakistan.'

QUESTION 2   Why did the Huguenots come to Britain?

 ☐ **A**   To invade the country and seize land

 ☐ **B**   To find jobs and a better life

 ☐ **C**   To avoid religious persecution

 ☐ **D**   To avoid a famine

QUESTION 3   Which of these statements is correct?

 ☐ **A**   In the 1950s, centres were set up in the West Indies to recruit bus drivers for the UK.

 ☐ **B**   n the 1950s, centres were set up in India and Pakistan to recruit bus drivers for the UK.

QUESTION 4   Is the statement below   ☐ TRUE or ☐ FALSE?

 'After the Second World War the British government invited people from Ireland and other parts of Europe to come to the UK.'

QUESTION 5   Since 1979 the number of refugees from South East Asia who have been allowed to settle in the UK is:

 ☐ **A**   Less than 2,500

 ☐ **B**   Between 2,501 and 10,000

 ☐ **C**   Between 10,001 and 25,000

 ☐ **D**   Over 25,000

QUESTION 6   Is the statement below   ☐ TRUE or ☐ FALSE?

 'In the UK, boys leave school on average with better qualifications than girls.'

QUESTION 7   Women in Britain first got the vote in:

☐ **A**   1882

☐ **B**   1918

☐ **C**   1928

☐ **D**   1945

QUESTION 8   Is the statement below   ☐ TRUE or ☐ FALSE?

'In the UK, it is illegal to discriminate against women at work because of their sex.'

QUESTION 9   From which TWO places were people invited to come and work in the UK during the 1950s?

☐ **A**   India

☐ **B**   New Zealand

☐ **C**   Russia

☐ **D**   West Indies

QUESTION 10   Is the statement below   ☐ TRUE or ☐ FALSE?

'Women have had equal voting rights with men in the UK since 1928'.

QUESTION 11   In which year did married women get the right to divorce their husband?

☐ **A**   1837

☐ **B**   1857

☐ **C**   1875

☐ **D**   1882

QUESTION 12   Jewish people came to Britain from Poland, Ukraine and Belarus to escape racist attacks

☐ **A**   from 1830 to 1850

☐ **B**   from 1880 to 1910

☐ **C**   from 1910 to 1920

☐ **D**   from 1930 to 1945

QUESTION 13   The Irish famine was in the middle of the

☐ **A**   1820s
☐ **B**   1830s
☐ **C**   1840s
☐ **D**   1850s

QUESTION 14   Is the statement below   ☐ TRUE or ☐ FALSE?

'In the late 1960s the government passed new laws which restricted immigration from Australia, New Zealand and Canada.'

QUESTION 15   In the late 19th and early 20th centuries, many women demonstrated for what right?

☐ **A**   The right to vote
☐ **B**   The right to equal pay
☐ **C**   The right to divorce their husbands
☐ **D**   The right to have an abortion

QUESTION 16   What percentage of the UK workforce are women?

☐ **A**   43%
☐ **B**   45%
☐ **C**   49%
☐ **D**   51%

QUESTION 17   Is the statement below   ☐ TRUE or ☐ FALSE?

'There are 2 million children at work in the UK at any one time.'

QUESTION 18   The proportion of young people who go on to higher education in the UK is

☐ **A**   1 in 2
☐ **B**   1 in 3
☐ **C**   1 in 4
☐ **D**   1 in 5

QUESTION 19 Is this statement ☐ TRUE or ☐ FALSE?

'Children often start part-time work when they are 11 years old.'

QUESTION 20 Which TWO examinations do young people take at 16?

☐ **A** GCSE

☐ **B** AGCE

☐ **C** SQA standard grade

☐ **D** SQA higher grade

QUESTION 21 A 'gap year' describes

☐ **A** the school summer holidays

☐ **B** a year that students spend working in industry

☐ **C** a year between school and university which students spend travelling or working

☐ **D** the year after GCSEs

QUESTION 22 Young people can vote in the UK from the age of

☐ **A** 17

☐ **B** 18

☐ **C** 19

☐ **D** 20

QUESTION 23 Is this statement ☐ TRUE or ☐ FALSE?

'It is against the law to be drunk in a public place in the UK.'

QUESTION 24 The number of children and young people up to the age of 19 in the UK is

☐ **A** 13 million

☐ **B** 14 million

☐ **C** 15 million

☐ **D** 16 million

QUESTION 25   A 'suffragette' was

    ☐ **A**   a woman who suffered persecution

    ☐ **B**   a woman who demonstrated for greater rights

    ☐ **C**   a woman who worked during the First World War

    ☐ **D**   a woman who stayed at home to raise her family

QUESTION 26   In the UK, children must attend school until they are

    ☐ **A**   14 years old

    ☐ **B**   15 years old

    ☐ **C**   16 years old

    ☐ **D**   17 years old

QUESTION 27   In the 1950s, textile and engineering firms sent agents to which TWO countries to find workers?

    ☐ **A**   Russia

    ☐ **B**   India

    ☐ **C**   Vietnam

    ☐ **D**   Pakistan

QUESTION 28   Is the statement below   ☐ TRUE or ☐ FALSE?

'The number of people migrating to Britain from the West Indies, India, Pakistan and Bangladesh increased during the late 1960s and early 1970s.'

QUESTION 29   Is the statement below   ☐ TRUE or ☐ FALSE?

'In the UK, women are often asked by employers to leave their jobs when they get married.'

QUESTION 30   By what percentage is the average hourly pay of women lower than men's?

    ☐ **A**   5%

    ☐ **B**   10%

    ☐ **C**   15%

    ☐ **D**   20%

QUESTION 31   What percentage of children live with only one parent?

☐ **A**   13%

☐ **B**   18%

☐ **C**   22%

☐ **D**   25%

QUESTION 32   Children in England and Scotland take national tests

☐ **A**   at 7, 12 and 16

☐ **B**   at 11, 16 and 18

☐ **C**   at 7, 11 and 14

☐ **D**   at 7, 12 and 14

QUESTION 33   Which of these statements is correct?

☐ **A**   It is illegal to sell tobacco products to anyone under 16 years of age.

☐ **B**   It is illegal to sell tobacco products to anyone under 18 years of age.

QUESTION 34   Is the statement below   ☐ TRUE or ☐ FALSE?

'There are more women than men in Britain.'

QUESTION 35   How many women with children at school are in paid work?

☐ **A**   Nearly a quarter

☐ **B**   Nearly a half

☐ **C**   Nearly two-thirds

☐ **D**   Nearly three-quarters

QUESTION 36   The initials GCSE stand for

☐ **A**   Graduate Certificate of Secondary Education

☐ **B**   General Certificate of Special Education

☐ **C**   General Certificate of Secondary Education

☐ **D**   Grade Certificate of School Education

QUESTION 37 What proportion of the population of Britain have used illegal drugs at one time?

☐ **A** About a tenth
☐ **B** About a quarter
☐ **C** About a third
☐ **D** About a half

QUESTION 38 Is the statement below ☐ TRUE or ☐ FALSE?

'Half of young people have taken part in fundraising or collecting money for charity.'

QUESTION 39 In the 2001 general election, how many first-time voters used their vote?

☐ **A** 1 in 4
☐ **B** 1 in 5
☐ **C** 1 in 10
☐ **D** 1 in 3

QUESTION 40 AS levels are gained by completing

☐ **A** three AS units
☐ **B** four AS units
☐ **C** three GCSEs
☐ **D** four GCSEs

Answers and pointers to questions on Chapter 2

Question	Answer	Reference (page number in *Life in the UK: A Journey to Citizenship*)	Notes
1	False	28	In the 1980s, the largest immigrant groups were from the United States, Australia, South Africa and New Zealand.
2	C	27	In the 16th and 18th centuries, Huguenots came to Britain to escape religious persecution in France.
3	A	27	
4	True	27	
5	D	28	
6	False	29	These days, girls leave school with better qualifications than boys.
7	B	29	In 1918, women over 30 were given the right to vote. In 1928, women won the right to vote at 21, the same age as men.
8	True	29	During the 1960s and 1970s, Parliament passed new laws giving women the right to equal pay and prohibiting employers from discriminating against women because of their sex.
9	A and D	27/28	
10	True	29	In 1918, women over 30 were given the right to vote. In 1928, women won the right to vote at 21, the same age as men.
11	B	29	Until 1857, a married woman had no right to divorce her husband.
12	B	27	From 1880 to 1910, a large number of Jewish people came to Britain to escape racist attacks (called 'pogroms') in what was then called the Russian Empire.
13	C	27	In the mid-1840s, there was a terrible famine in Ireland and many people migrated to Britain.

Question	Answer	Reference (page number in *Life in the UK: A Journey to Citizenship*)	Notes
14	False	28	In the late 1960s and early 1970s, the government passed new laws to restrict immigration to Britain although immigrants from 'old' Commonwealth countries such as Australia, New Zealand and Canada did not have to face such strict controls.
15	A	29	
16	B	29	
17	True	31	It is common for young people to have a part-time job while they are still at school.
18	B	31	
19	False	31	Children are not usually allowed to start work before they are 14 years old.
20	A and C	31	
21	C	31	
22	B	33	
23	True	32	
24	C	30	
25	B	29	In the late 19th and early 20th centuries, an increasing number of women campaigned and demonstrated for greater rights, and in particular the right to vote. They became known as 'suffragettes'.
26	C	30	
27	B and D	28	
28	False	28	The number of people migrating from these areas fell in the late 1960s and early 1970s because the government passed new laws to restrict immigration to Britain.

Question	Answer	Reference (page number in *Life in the UK: A Journey to Citizenship*)	Notes
29	False	29	Earlier in the 20th century it was common for employers to ask women to leave their jobs when they got married, but later Parliament passed new laws prohibiting employers from discriminating against women.
30	D	29	
31	D	30	
32	C	30	
33	B	31	
34	True	29	Women make up 51% of the population.
35	D	29	
36	C	31	
37	C	32	
38	True	33	
39	B	33	
40	A	31	

Chapter 3
UK TODAY: A PROFILE

This chapter provides a summary of the content of Chapter 3 of *Life in the United Kingdom: A Journey to Citizenship* and a set of test questions which will help you to examine your understanding of the chapter.

Summary of the chapter content

The population of the UK

- Gives facts about the size of the UK population and how it is changing.

The census

- Describes how the census is carried out, the information it collects, and how the information is used.

Ethnic diversity

- Gives details of the proportion of different ethnic groups within the UK and where they are located.

The nations and regions of Britain

- Describes the size of the UK and how it is divided into different nations and regions.

Religion and religious freedom

- Discusses the different religions present in the UK, the percentages of the population who practise them, the structure of the Christian churches in the UK, and the patron saints of England, Wales, Scotland and Northern Ireland.

Customs and traditions

- Describes the festivals and traditions celebrated within the UK and the UK's major sports and sporting events.

Questions to test your understanding of Chapter 3: UK Today: A Profile

---

QUESTION 1   In 2001 the population of the UK was nearly

- ☐ **A**   56 million
- ☐ **B**   58 million
- ☐ **C**   60 million
- ☐ **D**   62 million

QUESTION 2   Which TWO of the following statistics does the census collect?

- ☐ **A**   Age
- ☐ **B**   Height
- ☐ **C**   Weight
- ☐ **D**   Occupation

QUESTION 3   Is the following statement   ☐ TRUE or ☐ FALSE?

'There are more children under 16 in Britain than people over 60.'

QUESTION 4   In 2001, ethnic minority groups made up

- ☐ **A**   less than 5% of the population of England
- ☐ **B**   between 5 and 10% of the population of England
- ☐ **C**   between 10 and 15% of the population of England
- ☐ **D**   over 15% of the population of England

QUESTION 5   Which of the following statements is correct?

- ☐ **A**   The Geordie dialect is spoken in Tyneside.
- ☐ **B**   The Geordie dialect is spoken in Liverpool.

QUESTION 6   Is the following statement   ☐ TRUE or ☐ FALSE?

'The population of the North West of England has increased in recent years.'

QUESTION 7   St Andrew is the patron saint of which country?

☐ **A**   England

☐ **B**   Scotland

☐ **C**   Wales

☐ **D**   Northern Ireland

QUESTION 8   The percentage of the population who attend religious services in the UK is

☐ **A**   5%

☐ **B**   10%

☐ **C**   15%

☐ **D**   20%

QUESTION 9   Is the following statement   ☐ TRUE or ☐ FALSE?

'In the UK, 1st April is a day when people play jokes on each other.'

QUESTION 10   When will the next census be taken?

☐ **A**   2010

☐ **B**   2011

☐ **C**   2012

☐ **D**   2013

QUESTION 11   Is the following statement   ☐ TRUE or ☐ FALSE?

'The monarch of the UK is not allowed to marry anyone who is not Protestant.'

QUESTION 12   The 31st October celebrates

☐ **A**   Valentine's Day

☐ **B**   Guy Fawkes' night

☐ **C**   Hallowe'en

☐ **D**   Hogmanay

QUESTION 13   Is the following statement   ☐ TRUE or ☐ FALSE?

'The UK football team is very important to British people.'

QUESTION 14   The Notting Hill Carnival is held in

☐ **A**   Liverpool

☐ **B**   Manchester

☐ **C**   Edinburgh

☐ **D**   London

QUESTION 15   Is the following statement   ☐ TRUE or ☐ FALSE?

'Ulster Scots is a dialect which is spoken in Northern Ireland.'

QUESTION 16   Which TWO of these are names for the Church of England?

☐ **A**   Methodist

☐ **B**   Episcopal

☐ **C**   Anglican

☐ **D**   Presbyterian

QUESTION 17   When do people in the UK wear poppies?

☐ **A**   New Year

☐ **B**   Valentine's Day

☐ **C**   Remembrance Day

☐ **D**   Mother's Day

QUESTION 18   Is the following statement   ☐ TRUE or ☐ FALSE?

'Everyone in the UK has the legal right to practise the religion of their choice.'

QUESTION 19   Which TWO of the following are public holidays in England?

☐ **A**   1st January

☐ **B**   2nd January

☐ **C**   31st October

☐ **D**   26th December

QUESTION 20   The head of the Church of England is

☐ **A**   the Archbishop of Canterbury

☐ **B**   the Prime Minister

☐ **C**   the Queen

☐ **D**   the Moderator

QUESTION 21   The Grand National is a

☐ **A**   horse race

☐ **B**   tennis tournament

☐ **C**   football match

☐ **D**   cricket match

QUESTION 22   The 14th February celebrates

☐ **A**   Valentine's Day

☐ **B**   Guy Fawkes' night

☐ **C**   Hallowe'en

☐ **D**   Hogmanay

QUESTION 23   The population of Scotland is just over

☐ **A**   1 million

☐ **B**   3 million

☐ **C**   5 million

☐ **D**   7 million

QUESTION 24 Which of the following statements is correct?

☐ **A**   Information in the census is immediately available for the public to search.

☐ **B**   Information in the census is kept secret for 100 years.

QUESTION 25 The percentage of people in the UK in 2001 who said they were Muslims was

☐ **A**   1.6%

☐ **B**   2.7%

☐ **C**   3.4%

☐ **D**   4.2%

QUESTION 26 Which of the following statements is correct?

☐ **A**   Fireworks are traditionally set off on 31st October in the UK.

☐ **B**   Fireworks are traditionally set off on 5th November in the UK.

QUESTION 27 Is the following statement   ☐ TRUE or ☐ FALSE?

'At school, children learn about customs and traditions from various religions such as Eid-ul-Fitr, Diwali and Hannukah.'

QUESTION 28 The percentage of Black or Black British people in the UK in 2001 was

☐ **A**   2%

☐ **B**   4%

☐ **C**   5%

☐ **D**   7%

QUESTION 29 Gaelic is spoken in which TWO countries in the UK?

☐ **A**   England

☐ **B**   Wales

☐ **C**   Scotland

☐ **D**   Northern Ireland

QUESTION 30   Is the following statement   ☐ TRUE or ☐ FALSE?

'Every household in the UK is required by law to complete a census form.'

QUESTION 31   Is the following statement   ☐ TRUE or ☐ FALSE?

'More people attend religious services in England and Wales than in Scotland and Northern Ireland.'

QUESTION 32   St Patrick's Day is celebrated on

☐ **A**   1st March

☐ **B**   17th March

☐ **C**   23rd April

☐ **D**   30th November

QUESTION 33   On Christmas Day, people in the UK usually

☐ **A**   stay at home and eat a special meal

☐ **B**   spend the day fasting

☐ **C**   go to work

☐ **D**   go shopping

QUESTION 34   The Scouse dialect is spoken in

☐ **A**   London

☐ **B**   Liverpool

☐ **C**   Tyneside

☐ **D**   Wales

QUESTION 35   Hogmanay is traditionally celebrated in

☐ **A**   England

☐ **B**   Wales

☐ **C**   Scotland

☐ **D**   Northern Ireland

QUESTION 36 Is the following statement ☐ TRUE or ☐ FALSE?

'There are twice as many Hindus as Jews in the UK.'

QUESTION 37 Which of the following statements is true?

☐ **A** 45% of all ethnic minority people in the UK live in London.

☐ **B** 35% of all ethnic minority people in the UK live in London.

QUESTION 38 What percentage of the population of the UK live in England?

☐ **A** 65%

☐ **B** 72%

☐ **C** 76%

☐ **D** 84%

QUESTION 39 Baptists are a type of

☐ **A** Protestant Christian

☐ **B** Roman Catholic

☐ **C** Muslim

☐ **D** Jew

QUESTION 40 The number of Bank Holidays every year is

☐ **A** 2

☐ **B** 3

☐ **C** 4

☐ **D** 5

Answers and pointers to questions on Chapter 3

Question	Answer	Reference (page number in *Life in the UK: A Journey to Citizenship*)	Notes
1	C	35	
2	A and D	35	
3	False	35	
4	B	37	In England, ethnic minority groups make up 9% of the total population.
5	A	37	Well-known dialects in England are Geordie (Tyneside), Scouse (Liverpool) and Cockney (London).
6	False	35	Although the general population of the UK has increased in the last 20 years, in some areas such as the North East and North West of England, there has been a decline.
7	B	39	St Andrew is the patron saint of Scotland.
8	B	38	
9	True	40	
10	B	36	
11	True	39	
12	C	41	
13	False	41	There are no UK teams for football and rugby. England, Scotland, Wales and Northern Ireland have their own teams.
14	D	40	The Notting Hill Carnival is held in west London.
15	True	37	
16	B and C	39	The Church of England is called the Anglican Church in other countries and the Episcopal Church in Scotland.

Question	Answer	Reference (page number in *Life in the UK: A Journey to Citizenship*)	Notes
17	C	41	Many people wear poppies on Remembrance Day in memory of those who died fighting in the First World War.
18	True	38	Although the UK is historically a Christian society, everyone has the legal right to practise the religion of their choice.
19	A and D	40	1st January is a public holiday in the whole of the UK. 2nd January is a public holiday only in Scotland.
20	C	39	The king or queen is the head, or Supreme Governor, of the Church of England.
21	A	41	
22	A	40	
23	C	35	The population of Scotland was 5.1 million in 2005.
24	B	36	Census information remains confidential and anonymous; it can only be released to the public after 100 years.
25	B	38	
26	B	41	
27	True	40	
28	A	36	In the 2001 census, there were 1% Black Caribbean, 0.8% Black African and 0.2% Black Other people (1% + 0.8% + 0.2% = 2%)
29	C and D	37	
30	True	36	
31	False	38	
32	B	39	St Patrick's Day is celebrated in Northern Ireland on 17th March.
33	A	40	

Question	Answer	Reference (page number in *Life in the UK: A Journey to Citizenship*)	Notes
34	B	37	
35	C	40	In Scotland, 31st December is called Hogmanay and is a bigger holiday for some people than Christmas.
36	True	38	1% of the population is Hindu and 0.5% of the population is Jewish.
37	A	37	
38	D	35	
39	A	39	
40	C	39	There are four Bank Holidays and four other public holidays a year.

Chapter 4
HOW THE UK IS GOVERNED

This chapter provides a summary of the content of Chapter 4 of *Life in the United Kingdom: A Journey to Citizenship* and a set of test questions which will help you to examine your understanding of the chapter.

Summary of the chapter content

The British constitution

- Describes the system of government, including the roles of and the relationship between the monarchy and the government; the electoral system and voting rights; the political parties and the Houses of Parliament; the devolved parliaments; local government, the judiciary and the police

The UK in Europe and the world

- Describes the UK's relationship with and the roles of the Commonwealth, the European Union, the Council of Europe and the United Nations.

Questions to test your understanding of Chapter 4: How the UK is Governed

QUESTION 1   The heir to the throne is

- ☐ **A**   Princess Anne
- ☐ **B**   Prince Charles
- ☐ **C**   Prince Philip
- ☐ **D**   Prince William

QUESTION 2   Which TWO of the following constitute Parliament?

- ☐ **A**   The House of Commons
- ☐ **B**   The Cabinet
- ☐ **C**   The House of Lords
- ☐ **D**   The civil service

QUESTION 3   Is the following statement   ☐ TRUE or ☐ FALSE?

'The monarch of the UK makes decisions on government policies.'

QUESTION 4   The Chancellor of the Exchequer is responsible for

- ☐ **A**   education
- ☐ **B**   law and order
- ☐ **C**   health
- ☐ **D**   the economy

QUESTION 5   Which of the following statements is correct?

- ☐ **A**   Anyone can stand for election to the UK Parliament.
- ☐ **B**   Only those who have been nominated to represent a political party can stand for election to the UK Parliament.

QUESTION 6   Is the following statement   ☐ TRUE or ☐ FALSE?

'In the UK, a judge decides whether someone is guilty or innocent of a serious crime.'

QUESTION 7   In which TWO of the following places does the European Parliament meet?

- ☐ **A**   London
- ☐ **B**   Strasbourg
- ☐ **C**   Paris
- ☐ **D**   Brussels

QUESTION 8   Elections in the UK have to be held at least every

- ☐ **A**   3 years
- ☐ **B**   4 years
- ☐ **C**   5 years
- ☐ **D**   6 years

QUESTION 9   Is the following statement   ☐ TRUE or ☐ FALSE?

'The UK has a written constitution.'

QUESTION 10   Which of the following countries is NOT a member of the Commonwealth?

- ☐ **A**   Mozambique
- ☐ **B**   Seychelles
- ☐ **C**   Singapore
- ☐ **D**   Indonesia

QUESTION 11   Is the following statement   ☐ TRUE or ☐ FALSE?

'The Government cannot instruct the police what to do in any particular case.'

QUESTION 12   Which of the following countries does NOT operate a system of proportional representation?

- ☐ **A**   England
- ☐ **B**   Wales
- ☐ **C**   Scotland
- ☐ **D**   Northern Ireland

QUESTION 13   Is the following statement   ☐ TRUE or ☐ FALSE?

'Members of the public may not attend debates in the Houses of Parliament.'

QUESTION 14   A quango is

☐ **A**   a government department

☐ **B**   a non-departmental public body

☐ **C**   an arm of the judiciary

☐ **D**   an educational establishment

QUESTION 15   Is the following statement   ☐ TRUE or ☐ FALSE?

'Citizens of an EU member state have the right to travel and work in any EU country.'

QUESTION 16   Which TWO of the following are members of the Cabinet?

☐ **A**   The Chancellor of the Exchequer

☐ **B**   The Speaker of the House of Commons

☐ **C**   The Leader of the Opposition

☐ **D**   The Home Secretary

QUESTION 17   How many parliamentary constituencies are there?

☐ **A**   464

☐ **B**   564

☐ **C**   646

☐ **D**   664

QUESTION 18   Is the following statement   ☐ TRUE or ☐ FALSE?

'Discipline in the parliamentary parties is carried out by a group of people called the Whips.'

QUESTION 19   Which TWO of the following can vote in all UK public elections?

- [ ] **A**   Citizens of the Irish Republic resident in the UK
- [ ] **B**   Citizens of EU states resident in the UK
- [ ] **C**   Citizens of the Commonwealth resident in the UK
- [ ] **D**   Anyone resident in the UK

QUESTION 20   The initials MEP stand for

- [ ] **A**   Member Elected to Parliament
- [ ] **B**   Member of the Edinburgh Parliament
- [ ] **C**   Member of the European Parliament
- [ ] **D**   Member of the Executive Parliament

QUESTION 21   The official report of the proceedings of Parliament is called

- [ ] **A**   the Speaker's notes
- [ ] **B**   Hansard
- [ ] **C**   the electoral register
- [ ] **D**   the constitution

QUESTION 22   Where is the Prime Minister's official residence?

- [ ] **A**   Chequers
- [ ] **B**   10 Downing Street
- [ ] **C**   11 Downing Street
- [ ] **D**   Buckingham Palace

QUESTION 23   Who has the task of applying the Human Rights Act?

- [ ] **A**   The House of Commons
- [ ] **B**   The police
- [ ] **C**   The House of Lords
- [ ] **D**   The judiciary

QUESTION 24 Which of the following statements is correct?

☐ **A**   The UK was a founder member of the European Economic Community.

☐ **B**   The UK was a founder member of the Council of Europe.

QUESTION 25 How many countries are there in the European Union?

☐ **A**   6

☐ **B**   15

☐ **C**   25

☐ **D**   27

QUESTION 26 Which of the following statements is correct?

☐ **A**   Civil servants have to be members of the political party of the government they serve.

☐ **B**   Civil servants have to be politically neutral and professional.

QUESTION 27 Is the following statement ☐ TRUE or ☐ FALSE?

'The Welsh Assembly is responsible for taxation in Wales.'

QUESTION 28 How many seats does the UK hold in the European Parliament?

☐ **A**   58

☐ **B**   68

☐ **C**   78

☐ **D**   88

QUESTION 29 The legal voting age in the UK is

☐ **A**   16

☐ **B**   18

☐ **C**   20

☐ **D**   21

QUESTION 30 Is the following statement ☐ TRUE or ☐ FALSE?

'People who rent properties do not have to pay council tax.'

QUESTION 31 Is the following statement ☐ TRUE or ☐ FALSE?

'All members of both Houses of Parliament are democratically elected.'

QUESTION 32 The aims of the United Nations are

☐ **A**   to function as a single market

☐ **B**   to prevent war and promote peace and security

☐ **C**   to examine decisions made by the European Union

☐ **D**   to promote democracy, good government and eradicate poverty

QUESTION 33 The group of senior MPs appointed by the Leader of the Opposition to lead the criticism of government ministers is called:

☐ **A**   the Opposition Cabinet

☐ **B**   the shadow ministers

☐ **C**   the Shadow Cabinet

☐ **D**   the Opposition ministers

QUESTION 34 Life peers are appointed by

☐ **A**   the monarch

☐ **B**   the Prime Minister

☐ **C**   the Speaker of the House of Commons

☐ **D**   the Chief Whip

QUESTION 35 In order to vote in an election you must have

☐ **A**   a UK passport

☐ **B**   your name on the electoral register

☐ **C**   an identity card

☐ **D**   a place to live

QUESTION 36   Is the following statement   ☐ TRUE or ☐ FALSE?

'The Government can control what is written in newspapers in the UK.'

QUESTION 37   Which of the following statements is true?

☐ **A**   The governing body of the EU is the Council of the European Union.

☐ **B**   The governing body of the EU is the Council of Europe.

QUESTION 38   A by-election is held

☐ **A**   half-way through the life of a Parliament

☐ **B**   every two years

☐ **C**   when an MP dies or resigns

☐ **D**   when the Prime Minister decides to call one

QUESTION 39   Prime Minister's Questions take place

☐ **A**   every day when Parliament is sitting

☐ **B**   every week when Parliament is sitting

☐ **C**   every fortnight when Parliament is sitting

☐ **D**   once per month when Parliament is sitting

QUESTION 40   The Scottish Parliament meets at

☐ **A**   Holyrood

☐ **B**   Holywood

☐ **C**   Holywell

☐ **D**   Holyhead

Answers and pointers to questions on Chapter 4

Question	Answer	Reference (page number in *Life in the UK: A Journey to Citizenship*)	Notes
1	B	44	Prince Charles, the Queen's oldest son, is the heir to the throne.
2	A and C	43	
3	False	43	The king or queen does not rule the country but appoints the Government and the decisions on government policies are made by the Prime Minister and Cabinet.
4	D	45	
5	A	46	
6	False	48	Judges cannot decide whether people are guilty or innocent of a serious crime. When someone is accused of a serious crime, a jury decides whether he or she is innocent or guilty, and if guilty the judge will decide on the penalty.
7	B and D	53	
8	C	44	
9	False	41	The British constitution is not written down.
10	D	52	
11	True	49	The police have operational independence which means that the Government cannot instruct them what to do in any particular case.
12	A	44 and 47	In England MPs are elected in a system called 'first past the post' where the candidate who gets the most votes is elected and the Government is formed by the party which wins the majority of constituencies.
13	False	50	The public can listen to debates in the Palace of Westminster from public galleries both in the House of Commons and in the House of Lords.

Question	Answer	Reference (page number in *Life in the UK: A Journey to Citizenship*)	Notes
14	B	49	
15	True	52	
16	A and D	45	
17	C	44	
18	True	44	
19	A and C	49	All UK-born and naturalised citizens have the right to vote in all public elections, as do citizens of the Commonwealth and the Irish republic if resident in the UK.
20	C	45	
21	B	49	
22	B	45	
23	D	48	
24	B	52/53	The UK did not join the EEC until 1973, but was a founder member of the Council of Europe when it was created in 1949.
25	D	52	
26	B	47	
27	False	47	Policy and laws governing defence, foreign affairs, taxation and social security remain under central government control.
28	C	44	
29	B	49	
30	False	48	Council tax applies to all domestic properties whether owned or rented.
31	False	45	Members of the House of Lords are not elected. They either inherit their place in the House of Lords, are senior judges or bishops of the Church of England, or are Life Peers appointed by a Prime Minister.

Question	Answer	Reference (page number in *Life in the UK: A Journey to Citizenship*)	Notes
32	B	53	
33	C	46	
34	A	45	Life Peers are appointed by the Queen on the advice of the Prime Minister.
35	B	49	
36	False	49	The UK has a free press which means that what is written in newspapers is free of government control.
37	A	52	
38	C	44	
39	B	46	
40	A	51	

Chapter 5
EVERYDAY NEEDS

This chapter provides a summary of the content of Chapter 5 of *Life in the United Kingdom: A Journey to Citizenship* and a set of test questions which will help you to examine your understanding of the chapter.

Summary of the chapter content

Housing

- Discusses the processes and agents involved in buying and renting a home; homelessness and how to get help.

Services in and for the home

- Information about the provision and payment for utilities and local government services; council tax; buildings and household insurance; problems with neighbours and mediation services.

Money and credit

- Discusses how money and credit work in the UK, including dealing with banks and building societies; cash, credit, debit and store cards; credit and loans; and social security benefits.

Health

- Discusses how to use the NHS including finding and registering with a doctor, dentist or optician; what to do when you feel unwell and in cases of emergencies; who has to pay prescription charges; pregnancy and care of young children; registering a birth.

Education

- Discusses types of schools and costs; going to school and parents' responsibilities; the curriculum and assessment; further education establishments

Leisure

- Covers the rules regarding leisure activities, such as video and DVD classification; TV and radio licences; the age at which you can go into pubs, night clubs, betting shops and gambling clubs; and your responsibilities if you own a pet.

Travel and transport

- Discusses public transport and the rules and regulations concerning owning and driving a motor vehicle.

Identity documents

- Occasions when you may be asked to prove your identity and how to do so.

Questions to test your understanding of Chapter 5: Everyday Needs

QUESTION 1   Is the statement below   ☐ TRUE or ☐ FALSE?

'People who buy their own homes usually pay for it with a mortgage, which is a
loan from a bank or building society usually paid back over 15 years.'

QUESTION 2   Why should you use a solicitor when buying a property?

☐ **A**   They check that the property is structurally sound.

☐ **B**   They carry out legal checks on the property, the seller and the local area.

☐ **C**   They negotiate the repayment terms of your mortgage with the bank or building society.

☐ **D**   They act on behalf of both buyer and seller.

QUESTION 3   Which of these statements is correct?

☐ **A**   When renting a property a deposit is paid to the landlord at the beginning of the tenancy to cover the cost of any damage.

☐ **B**   When renting a property a deposit is paid to the landlord at the beginning of the tenancy to cover his/her administrative costs.

QUESTION 4   Approximately what proportion of people in the UK own their own home?

☐ **A**   One-third

☐ **B**   One-quarter

☐ **C**   One-half

☐ **D**   Two-thirds

QUESTION 5   Is the statement below   ☐ TRUE or ☐ FALSE?

'If you apply for council housing, you will be assessed according to need using a system of
points. You get more points if you are homeless, have children, or are chronically ill.'

QUESTION 6   How are water rates billed?

☐ **A**   They are included in your council tax.

☐ **B**   They are billed either as one payment (lump sum) or a series
of instalments.

QUESTION 7   Which of these statements is correct?

☐ **A**   The amount of council tax you pay depends on how many people live in
the property.

☐ **B**   The amount of council tax you pay depends on the size and value of
your property.

QUESTION 8   Who is responsible for the collection and disposal of waste?

☐ **A**   The owner of the property

☐ **B**   The residents' association

☐ **C**   The local authority

☐ **D**   The Government

QUESTION 9   Is the statement below   ☐ TRUE or ☐ FALSE?

*'If you have problems with your neighbours, you should contact the police for
details of mediation organisations that can help solve disputes.'*

QUESTION 10   What insurance is compulsory for the following items?

☐ **A**   Credit cards

☐ **B**   Health

☐ **C**   Car or motorcycle

☐ **D**   Mobile phones

QUESTION 11   Which of these statements is correct?

☐ **A**   A debit card does not draw money from your bank account, but you will be sent a bill every month.

☐ **B**   A store card is like a credit card but can be used only in a particular shop.

QUESTION 12   Which TWO items could you provide as documentation when opening a bank or building society account?

☐ **A**   A current passport

☐ **B**   A signed photograph

☐ **C**   Your birth certificate

☐ **D**   Tenancy agreement or household bill showing your address

QUESTION 13   Is the statement below   ☐ TRUE or ☐ FALSE?

'Credit unions are financial co-operatives owned and controlled by their members. Interest rates in credit unions are usually higher than in banks and building societies.'

QUESTION 14   Which of these statements is correct?

☐ **A**   Jobcentre Plus offices have information only for jobseekers.

☐ **B**   Jobcentre Plus offices have information for jobseekers and can provide information on welfare benefits.

QUESTION 15   Where do you register a birth?

☐ **A**   At the hospital where the birth took place

☐ **B**   At your GP's practice

☐ **C**   At the Register Office

☐ **D**   By calling NHS Direct

QUESTION 16 Which of the following TWO types of people get their prescriptions free of charge?

☐ **A** People aged 60 or over

☐ **B** People under 18 years of age

☐ **C** Pregnant women or those with a baby under 12 months old

☐ **D** People on the minimum wage

QUESTION 17 Is the statement below   ☐ TRUE or ☐ FALSE?

'You can attend a hospital without a GP's letter only in the case of an emergency.'

QUESTION 18 In which TWO places can you find the name of a dentist?

☐ **A** By enquiring at your GP's practice

☐ **B** By calling NHS Direct

☐ **C** By enquiring at a Citizens' Advice Bureau

☐ **D** By calling your local authority

QUESTION 19 Which of these statements is correct?

☐ **A** If you want to see a doctor you should call NHS Direct on 0845 46 47.

☐ **B** If you want to see a doctor you can make an appointment at your GP surgery or visit an NHS walk-in centre.

QUESTION 20 You can receive health advice and treatment when you are pregnant and after you have had the baby from which TWO sources?

☐ **A** Your GP

☐ **B** The Family Planning Association

☐ **C** Your health visitor

☐ **D** The local nursery

QUESTION 21 Is the statement below   ☐ TRUE or ☐ FALSE?

'Educational assessment in the UK is based on Key Stage tests at ages 7, 11 and 14.'

QUESTION 22   Who is responsible for making sure a child goes to school?

☐ **A**   The local education authority

☐ **B**   The headteacher of the school

☐ **C**   The parent or guardian of the child

☐ **D**   The local councillor

QUESTION 23   At what age do children in Scotland start secondary school?

☐ **A**   10

☐ **B**   12

☐ **C**   13

☐ **D**   14

QUESTION 24   Which of these statements is correct?

☐ **A**   Education at state schools in the UK is free and this includes the cost of school uniform and sports wear.

☐ **B**   Education at state schools in the UK is free but parents have to pay for school uniform and sports wear.

QUESTION 25   What TWO types of school are there in the UK in addition to state schools?

☐ **A**   Holy schools

☐ **B**   Independent schools

☐ **C**   Tertiary schools

☐ **D**   Faith schools

QUESTION 26   Schools must be open

☐ **A**   150 days a year

☐ **B**   170 days a year

☐ **C**   190 days a year

☐ **D**   200 days a year

QUESTION 27 Is the statement below ☐ TRUE or ☐ FALSE?

'Parents are excluded from membership of a school's governing body
which decides how the school is run and administered.'

QUESTION 28 Is the statement below ☐ TRUE or ☐ FALSE?

'Further education colleges only admit people up to the age of 19.'

QUESTION 29 Which of these statements is correct?

☐ **A** The National Curriculum covers English, maths and several other subjects but does not include modern foreign languages.

☐ **B** The National Curriculum covers English, maths and several other subjects including modern foreign languages.

QUESTION 30 Young people from families with low income can get financial help with their studies when they leave school at 16. This help is called

☐ **A** Education Support Grant

☐ **B** Further Learning and Training Support Allowance

☐ **C** Education Maintenance Allowance

☐ **D** Post-16 Education Allowance

QUESTION 31 Is the statement below ☐ TRUE or ☐ FALSE?

'To drink alcohol in a pub you must be 16 or over'.

QUESTION 32 What is the age requirement for someone wishing to see a PG classification film, video or DVD?

☐ **A** Suitable for all ages, but some parts may be unsuitable for children so parents should decide

☐ **B** Suitable for children 8 years and over if accompanied by an adult

☐ **C** Children under 15 years of age are not allowed to see or rent the film

☐ **D** Suitable for unaccompanied children 8 years and over

QUESTION 33   Which of these statements is correct?

☐ **A**   A TV licence covers all TV equipment at one address, even if people rent different rooms at that address.

☐ **B**   A TV licence covers all TV equipment at one address, but people who rent different rooms at that address must each buy a separate licence.

QUESTION 34   Which people are not allowed into betting shops or gambling clubs?

☐ **A**   People aged under 16

☐ **B**   People aged under 17

☐ **C**   People aged under 18

☐ **D**   People aged under 21

QUESTION 35   Is the statement below   ☐ TRUE or ☐ FALSE?

'It is a criminal offence to have a car without proper motor insurance and it is also illegal to allow someone to use your car if they are not insured to drive it.'

QUESTION 36   You must have a current MOT (Ministry of Transport) certificate for your car if it is over

☐ **A**   2 years old

☐ **B**   3 years old

☐ **C**   4 years old

☐ **D**   5 years old

QUESTION 37   Which of these statements is correct?

☐ **A**   For cars and motorcycles the speed limit on single carriageways is 60 mph.

☐ **B**   For cars and motorcycles the speed limit on single carriageways is 70 mph.

QUESTION 38 To drive a car or motorcycle in the UK, you must be at least:

- ☐ **A**   15 years old
- ☐ **B**   16 years old
- ☐ **C**   17 years old
- ☐ **D**   18 years old

QUESTION 39 Is the statement below   ☐ TRUE or ☐ FALSE?

'Driving away after an accident without stopping is a criminal offence.'

QUESTION 40 Which of these statements is correct?

- ☐ **A**   To open a bank account, you will need to provide proof of identity, such as a passport or National Insurance number card, and a document showing your name and current address, such as a recent utilities bill.
- ☐ **B**   To open a bank account, you will need to provide a document showing your name and current address, such as a recent utilities bill.

Answers and pointers to questions on Chapter 5

Question	Answer	Reference (page number in *Life in the UK: A Journey to Citizenship*)	Notes
1	False	55	The loan is normally paid back over 25 years.
2	B	56	
3	A	57	
4	D	55	
5	True	56	
6	B	58	
7	B	59	
8	C	58	
9	False	59	You can get details of mediation organisations from the local authority, Citizens' Advice and Mediation UK.
10	C	61	
11	B	60	
12	A and D	60	
13	False	61	Interest rates in credit unions are usually lower than in banks and building societies.
14	B	61	
15	C	65	
16	A and C	63	
17	True	62	
18	B and C	64	
19	B	63	
20	A and C	65	

Question	Answer	Reference (page number in *Life in the UK: A Journey to Citizenship*)	Notes
21	False	67	Educational assessment is carried out in England and Northern Ireland at 7, 11 and 14. In Wales, testing only takes place at 14, and in Scotland, teachers test children when they are ready.
22	C	66	
23	B	66	
24	B	66	
25	B and D	67	
26	C	68	
27	False	68	A number of places on school governing bodies are reserved for parents.
28	False	68	Most further education courses are free up to the age of 19 but further education colleges also offer courses for adults.
29	B	67	
30	C	68	
31	False	70	You must be 18 to drink alcohol in a pub. At 16 you can drink wine or beer with a meal in a hotel or restaurant.
32	A	69	
33	B	70	
34	C	70	
35	True	72	
36	B	72	
37	A	72	
38	C	71	
39	True	72	
40	A	73	

Chapter 6
EMPLOYMENT

This chapter provides a summary of the content of Chapter 6 of *Life in the UK: A Journey to Citizenship* and a set of test questions which will help you to examine your understanding of the chapter.

Summary of the chapter content

Looking for work and applying for jobs

- Covers who is allowed to work in the UK; compares overseas qualifications with UK qualifications; looks at how and where to find out where there are job vacancies; how to apply for jobs including the importance of CVs and referees; how the interview process works; and the checks carried out on those people who are likely to be working with vulnerable groups.

Training and volunteering

- Discusses where to find training and how training can help you to find work and the value of volunteering and work experience.

Equal rights and discrimination

- Outlines the rights and responsibilities of employers and employees; describes the Commission for Equality and Human Rights; and how to deal with sexual harassment.

Rights and responsibilities at work

- Explains the value of written contracts or statements and what they should include; helps you to understand tax, National Insurance and pensions; discusses health and safety issues at work; the trades unions; what happens when you lose your job, including redundancy and employment tribunals; and unemployment.

Working for yourself

- Discusses your responsibilities regarding tax and National Insurance; talks about sources of advice and information.

Childcare and children at work

- Describes maternal and paternal leave and benefits; the law regarding the employment of children; and employers' and parents' responsibilities.

Questions to test your understanding of Chapter 6: Employment

QUESTION 1 Is the statement below ☐ TRUE or ☐ FALSE?

'The Department of Work and Pensions provides guidance on who is allowed to work in the UK.'

QUESTION 2 Which TWO of the following types of people can act as your referee in support of a job application?

☐ **A** A family member

☐ **B** Your current or previous employer

☐ **C** Your college tutor

☐ **D** A personal friend

QUESTION 3 Which of these statements is correct?

☐ **A** The Home Office provides guidance on the applicability of overseas qualifications.

☐ **B** The National Academic Recognition Information Centre (NARIC) provides guidance on the applicability of overseas qualifications.

QUESTION 4 Choose TWO places from the list below where jobs are advertised.

☐ **A** Local library

☐ **B** Local jobcentre

☐ **C** Post Office

☐ **D** Local and national newspapers

QUESTION 5 Many job applications will require a covering letter and

☐ **A** a document showing proof of identity

☐ **B** your National Insurance number

☐ **C** a curriculum vitae

☐ **D** a signed photograph

QUESTION 6   Is the statement below   ☐ TRUE or ☐ FALSE?

'If you are applying for a job which involves working with vulnerable people, it will
be necessary for your employer to do a CRB (Criminal Records Bureau) check.'

QUESTION 7   Information about training opportunities can be found from which TWO
of the following?

☐ **A**   The local library
☐ **B**   The local council offices
☐ **C**   Learndirect
☐ **D**   The Home Office

QUESTION 8   Which of these statements is correct?

☐ **A**   If you are sexually harassed at work, you should tell a friend, colleague or
trade union representative and ask the person harassing you to stop.
☐ **B**   If you are sexually harassed at work, you should inform the
police immediately.

QUESTION 9   Advice and information on racial discrimination, sex discrimination and
disability issues can be obtained from

☐ **A**   your local jobcentre
☐ **B**   the Commission for Equality and Human Rights
☐ **C**   the Department for Work and Pensions
☐ **D**   your local library

QUESTION 10   Is the statement below   ☐ TRUE or ☐ FALSE?

'The minimum wage in the UK for workers aged 22 and above is £5.35 an hour.'

QUESTION 11 Your employer should give you a written contract or statement with all the details and conditions for your work within

☐ **A** 6 months of starting the job

☐ **B** 4 months of starting the job

☐ **C** 3 months of starting the job

☐ **D** 2 months of starting the job

QUESTION 12 Which of these statements is correct?

☐ **A** Most employees who are 16 or over are entitled to at least five weeks' paid holiday every year.

☐ **B** Most employees who are 16 or over are entitled to at least four weeks' paid holiday every year.

QUESTION 13 National Insurance (NI) contributions are used to help pay for which TWO of the following benefits?

☐ **A** State libraries

☐ **B** National Health Service

☐ **C** Universities

☐ **D** State Retirement Pension

QUESTION 14 Is the statement below   ☐ TRUE or ☐ FALSE?

'Your pay slip only shows how much money has been taken off for tax; it does not show National Insurance contributions.'

QUESTION 15 Which of these statements is correct?

☐ **A** You can apply for a National Insurance number by contacting HM Revenue and Customs.

☐ **B** You can apply for a National Insurance number through Jobcentre Plus or your local social security office.

QUESTION 16   The government department responsible for collecting taxes is

   ☐ **A**   the Department of Work and Pensions

   ☐ **B**   the Home Office

   ☐ **C**   HM Revenue and Customs

   ☐ **D**   the Central Office of Information

QUESTION 17   If you are self-employed, you are responsible for paying which TWO of the following?

   ☐ **A**   NI contributions

   ☐ **B**   NHS contributions

   ☐ **C**   State Retirement Pension contributions

   ☐ **D**   Your own tax

QUESTION 18   Is the statement below   ☐ TRUE or ☐ FALSE?

'Everyone who has paid enough National Insurance contributions will get a State Pension when they retire.'

QUESTION 19   The State Pension age is

   ☐ **A**   65 years for men and 60 for women

   ☐ **B**   70 years for men and 65 for women

   ☐ **C**   67 years for men and 62 for women

   ☐ **D**   72 years for men and 65 for women

QUESTION 20   Which of these statements is correct?

   ☐ **A**   You need a National Insurance number when you start work.

   ☐ **B**   You don't need a National Insurance number when you start work.

QUESTION 21   It is against the law for employers to discriminate against someone on the basis of which TWO factors from the list below:

☐ **A**   Weight

☐ **B**   Religion

☐ **C**   Height

☐ **D**   Sex

QUESTION 22   Is the statement below   ☐ TRUE or ☐ FALSE?

'Your employer can dismiss you for being a trade union member.'

QUESTION 23   Where can you find details of trade unions in the UK?

☐ **A**   The Home Office

☐ **B**   Local library

☐ **C**   Trades Union Congress (TUC) website

☐ **D**   Jobcentre Plus website

QUESTION 24   If you are worried about health and safety at your workplace you should

☐ **A**   make a report to the police

☐ **B**   write to the Department of Work and Pensions

☐ **C**   talk to your supervisor, manager or trade union representative

☐ **D**   contact a solicitor

QUESTION 25   Which of these statements is correct?

☐ **A**   Trade unions are organisations that aim to improve the pay and working conditions of their members.

☐ **B**   Trade unions are organisations that organise social events for their members.

QUESTION 26 From which TWO places can you obtain advice if you have a problem at work and need to take further action?

☐ **A** Citizens' Advice Bureau (CAB)

☐ **B** Your local MP

☐ **C** Your employer

☐ **D** The national Advisory, Conciliation and Arbitration Service (ACAS)

QUESTION 27 For which TWO reasons from the list below can an employer give you a warning?

☐ **A** You are overweight

☐ **B** You are unacceptably late for work

☐ **C** You cannot do your job properly

☐ **D** You are the wrong sex

QUESTION 28 Is the statement below   ☐ TRUE or ☐ FALSE?

'An employee can be dismissed immediately for serious misconduct at work.'

QUESTION 29 If you feel you have been unfairly dismissed from your job, you may be able to get compensation by taking your case to

☐ **A** the local Magistrates Court

☐ **B** the Home Office

☐ **C** an Employment Tribunal

☐ **D** HM Revenue and Customs

QUESTION 30 Which of these statements is correct?

☐ **A** If you lose your job because the company you work for no longer needs you, you may be entitled to an extra payment.

☐ **B** If you lose your job because the company you work for no longer needs you, you will not be entitled to any extra payment.

QUESTION 31 If you become unemployed, and are capable, available and trying to find work, you may be able to claim

☐ **A** an Education Support Grant

☐ **B** Jobseeker's Allowance

☐ **C** an Education Maintenance Allowance

☐ **D** a State Pension

QUESTION 32 Is the statement below   ☐ TRUE or ☐ FALSE?

'Adults who have been unemployed for six months are usually required to join New Deal if they wish to continue receiving benefit.'

QUESTION 33 Advice and information on setting up your own business is available from

☐ **A** jobcentres

☐ **B** solicitors

☐ **C** Business Link

☐ **D** your local library

QUESTION 34 Which of these statements is correct?

☐ **A** Women who are expecting a baby are entitled to at least 16 weeks' maternity leave.

☐ **B** Women who are expecting a baby are entitled to at least 26 weeks' maternity leave.

QUESTION 35 Fathers who have worked for their employer for at least 26 weeks are entitled to how many weeks' paternity leave?

☐ **A** 1 week

☐ **B** 3 weeks

☐ **C** 8 days

☐ **D** 2 weeks

QUESTION 36 Is the statement below ☐ TRUE or ☐ FALSE?

'Any child under school-leaving age (16) seeking to do paid work
must apply for a licence from the local authority.'

QUESTION 37 Legally, the earliest age children can work is

☐ **A** 12 years old
☐ **B** 14 years old
☐ **C** 16 years old
☐ **D** 13 years old

QUESTION 38 Which of these statements is correct?

☐ **A** Children aged 13–16 cannot work for more than 12 hours in any school week.
☐ **B** Children aged 13–16 cannot work for more than 10 hours in any school week.

QUESTION 39 Which TWO jobs from the following list are children aged under 16 not allowed to do?

☐ **A** Sell alcohol, cigarettes or medicines
☐ **B** Deliver newspapers
☐ **C** Work in a kitchen
☐ **D** Casual gardening

QUESTION 40 Is the statement below ☐ TRUE or ☐ FALSE?

'There is no national minimum wage for those under 16'.

Answers and pointers to questions on Chapter 6

Question	Answer	Reference (page number in *Life in the UK: A Journey to Citizenship*)	Notes
1	False	75	The Home Office provides guidance on work eligibility.
2	B and C	76	Personal friends and family members are not usually acceptable as referees.
3	B	75	
4	B and D	75	
5	C	76	
6	True	76	
7	A and C	76	
8	A	78	
9	B	78	
10	True	79	
11	D	79	
12	B	79	
13	B and D	80	
14	False	79	Pay slips should show both tax and NI contributions deducted.
15	B	80	
16	C	79	
17	A and D	82	
18	True	80	
19	A	80	
20	A	80	
21	B and D	77	

Question	Answer	Reference (page number in *Life in the UK: A Journey to Citizenship*)	Notes
22	False	81	
23	C	81	
24	C	80	
25	A	81	
26	A and D	81	
27	B and C	81	
28	True	81	
29	C	81	
30	A	81	
31	B	81	
32	False	82	You have to be unemployed for 18 months.
33	C	82	
34	B	84	
35	D	84	
36	True	84	
37	D	84	
38	A	84	
39	A and C	84	
40	True	85	

Appendix
A TEST TO ASSESS YOUR READING LEVEL

This information has been provided by the National Institute of Adult Continuing Education (NIACE). ESOL is an abbreviation for English for Speakers of Other Languages.

The following activity is to help you assess whether the level of your reading in English is at ESOL Entry 3 level.

The passage below is from a leaflet for parents with children at school. Read it and answer the questions. There is no time limit but try not to take more than about 45 minutes. You should not use a dictionary.

The questions are only to check your understanding of the language. They are like those in a Skills for Life ESOL test at Entry 3. **They are not the kind of questions that are in the Life in the UK Test**.

 Although the reading test provided by NIACE is at the right level, it is quite difficult to test your own English. If you have any doubts you should go to a local adult, further education or community college to ask for an assessment. Private colleges can also assess you, but you will have to pay for this.

School attendance, absence and your child

PARAGRAPH 1

If a child does not go to school regularly it can have a harmful effect on their future. For example, children who miss school frequently can fall behind with their work and fail their exams. A good school attendance record could show employers that your child is reliable. Research suggests that children who do not attend school regularly are more likely to get involved in antisocial behaviour or crime.

PARAGRAPH 2

All children between the ages of five and sixteen must receive a suitable full-time education. The majority of parents register their child at a school, though it is possible to make other arrangements, such as teaching them at home. After you have registered your child at a school, you are legally responsible for making sure they attend regularly. If your child does not do this, an education welfare officer, police officer or headteacher can give you a penalty notice. This means you will have to pay a fine. In very serious cases, a parent can be sent to prison for up to three months.

PARAGRAPH 3

You can help your child by:

- making sure they understand why they should attend regularly and punctually

- taking an interest in their education, for example by asking them about school work

- discussing any problems they may have at school and informing their teacher or headteacher about anything serious

- not letting them take time off school without a very good reason

You should always arrange appointments and outings after school hours, at weekends or during school holidays. Normally the school will not agree to your child going on holiday during term time.

PARAGRAPH 4

There are many possible reasons for a child not attending school. For example, other children may be bullying them. Or there may be difficulties with transport to and from school. If your child starts missing school, there may be a problem you do not know about. If you cannot solve the problem by talking to your child, you should make an appointment to see their teacher or form tutor. If there are more serious problems, such as long-term illness, an education welfare officer from your local authority may be able to provide support.

PARAGRAPH 5

If your child is missing school without a good reason, the school or local authority might ask you to sign a written agreement with them. This is known as a parenting contract. It means you agree to do certain things, for example, make sure that your child arrives at school punctually every day. Parenting contracts are voluntary. However, if you do refuse to agree to a contract, this can be used as evidence if the local authority decides to prosecute you.

(Adapted from information on the UK government website: www.direct.gov.uk)

Questions

QUESTION 1   In the third column, write the number of the paragraph that best matches each heading.

	Heading	Number
A	Support on school attendance	
B	School attendance and absence: the law	
C	Parenting contracts	
D	Regular school attendance: why it's so important	
E	Preventing your child from missing school: what you can do	

QUESTION 2   The leaflet gives both advice about what parents can do and information about the law. Which of the paragraphs gives advice and which gives information? Put a tick in the correct column. **One only** in each case.

Paragraph number	Advice	Information
1		
2		
3		
4		
5		

QUESTION 3   Read the sentences below and tick whether they are true or false.

		True	False
A	There is evidence that children who miss school may be more likely to get into trouble with the law.		
B	All children between the ages of 5 and 16 must go to school for their education.		
C	You will usually be able to take your child on a short holiday in term time.		
D	You must contact an education welfare officer if your child keeps missing school.		
E	You do not have to sign a parenting contract if you do not want to.		

QUESTION 4

A   In paragraph 1, which word means that *somebody can be trusted to work well*?

....

B   In paragraph 2, which word means *a punishment where you have to pay some money*?

....

C   In paragraph 3, which word means *at the right time*?

....

D   In paragraph 4, which word means *hurting or frightening somebody over a period of time*?

....

E   In paragraph 5, which word means *take somebody to court*?

....

QUESTION 5

A Name TWO people who, according to the leaflet, can give you a fine if your child does not attend school.

....

B According to the leaflet, who should you speak to first, if your child is missing school?

....

C Apart from bullying, what possible reason does the leaflet give for a child missing school?

....

D What example does the leaflet give of a problem that an education welfare officer can help you with?

....

Answers

Q1	A	4
	B	2
	C	5
	D	1
	E	3
Q2	1	Advice
	2	Information
	3	Advice
	4	Advice
	5	Information
Q3	A	True
	B	False
	C	False
	D	False
	E	True
Q4	A	Reliable
	B	Fine
	C	Punctually
	D	Bullying
	E	Prosecute
Q5	A	A headteacher, a police officer, an education welfare officer (two)
	B	Your child
	C	Difficulties with transport (to and from school)
	D	Long-term illness

Give one mark for each correct answer. There are a possible 24 marks. If you scored 18 or more, your level of reading is probably at Entry 3 or above. If you scored less than 18, you may have difficulty with the language of the handbook *Life in the UK: A Journey to Citizenship* and should consider taking a 'Skills for Life' ESOL course.

The course you attend must lead to an ESOL Skills for Life qualification and you should make sure that it also includes at least 20 hours of citizenship learning materials. If you achieve a qualification at Entry 1, Entry 2 or Entry 3 (it need only be in Speaking and Listening) on such a course, the provider will also give you a letter confirming that you learnt about citizenship topics. **You will not then have to take the Life in the UK Test**.

You must make sure that you take an exam set by one of the ESOL awarding bodies and not just a college exam in order to get a certificate that the UK Border Agency can accept.

Most further education colleges provide courses like this and a number of other organisations do also. Your local college will be able to advise you about the right class for you and tell you how much it will cost. Before you start a class, a tutor will probably assess you and advise you how long you are likely to need to attend before achieving the qualification.

Even if you passed this test easily, you could benefit from taking a more advanced ESOL course to improve particular skills, such as writing, as this might help you get a better job. It is possible to take ESOL courses up to Level 2, so it is worth finding out what is available in your area.

You can get more information about ESOL classes from the UK Government website: www.direct. gov.uk. The page that tells you about ESOL is:

http://www.direct.gov.uk/en/EducationAndLearning/AdultLearning/ImprovingYourSkills/ DG_10037499

This site also gives some helpline numbers that you can call to get advice. The main number is 0800 100 900 but there are also numbers where you can speak to an adviser in another language.

ADDITIONAL SOURCES
OF INFORMATION

The UK Border Agency

The UK Border Agency is the department of the Home Office which is responsible for considering applications for citizenship or permission to stay in the UK. They have two contact centres, the Immigration Enquiry Bureau (IEB) and the Nationality Contact Centre, which can provide helpful advice.

THE IMMIGRATION ENQUIRY BUREAU

The IEB can provide advice on leave to remain and settlement applications. Their contact details are:

Phone: 0870 606 7766
Textphone: 0800 389 8289
Email: UKBApublicenquiries@ind.homeoffice.gsi.gov.uk
Address: UK Border Agency,
                Lunar House,
                40 Wellesley Road,
                Croydon,
                Surrey CR9 2BY
Opening hours: Monday to Thursday 0900–1645, Friday 0900–1630

NATIONALITY CONTACT CENTRE

The Nationality Contact Centre can provide information on British citizenship and right of abode. Their contact details are:

Phone: 0845 010 5200
Email: nationalityenquiries@ind.homeoffice.gsi.gov.uk
Opening hours: Monday to Friday 0900–2100

NATIONALITY CHECKING SERVICE

The nationality checking service is provided by local authorities (for example, your county council or city council). The service allows you to make your application for British citizenship in person at your local council offices. A fee is charged for this service which is available from many, but not all, local authorities. If your local authority does not currently provide the service, you can go to another authority in your area. You can find the nearest nationality checking service at:

www.ukba.homeoffice.gov.uk/britishcitizenship/applying/checkingservice

Ufi, the organisation that runs the Life in the UK Test on behalf of the UK Border Agency, also provides information about the Life in the UK Test through the Life in the UK Test website: http://www.lifeintheuktest.gov.uk.

This provides a lot of information which will help you to prepare for the test.

You can also call the Life in the UK Test telephone helpline on 0800 015 4245. For help in another language, call the number listed below.

ਪੰਜਾਬੀ
0800 093 1333

সিলেটী
0800 093 1444

Soomali
0800 093 1555

polskim
0800 093 1114

français
0800 093 1115

فارسی
0800 093 1116

اردو
0800 093 1118

ગુજરાતી
0800 093 1119

UK online centres

UK online centres provide people with access to computers and the internet, together with help and advice on how to use them. You can find your nearest UK online centre by calling 0800 77 1234.

LearnDirect

LearnDirect operates more than 800 centres in England and Wales, where they provide courses to help you to improve your skills, including your English language skills. They provide courses which you can study at home, at work or at a Learndirect centre. To enquire about Learndirect courses, call the helpline on 0800 101 901.

Learndirect also provides helplines where you can speak to someone in your own language. The helplines are available from 0900 to 1700, Monday to Friday.

- Farsi   0800 0931116
- French   0800 093 1115
- Gujarati   0800 093 1119
- Punjabi   0800 093 1333
- Polish   0800 093 1114
- Somali   0800 093 1555
- Sylheti   0800 093 1444
- Urdu   0800 093 1118
- Welsh   0800 100 900

TSO (The Stationery Office)

TSO publishes *Life in the UK: A Journey to Citizenship*. You can buy the book from many bookshops or from their online bookshop http://www.tsoshop.co.uk

Life in the United Kingdom: A Journey to Citizenship
2nd Edition (2007)   9780113413133   £9.99

Life in the United Kingdom: A Journey to Citizenship
2nd Edition (2007) large print version   9780113413171   £9.99

Life in the United Kingdom: A Journey to Citizenship
2nd Edition (2007) PDF   9780113413232   £9.99 (£11.74 inc. VAT)

Life in the United Kingdom: A Journey to Citizenship
2nd Edition (2007) Audio CD   9780113413188   £9.99 (£11.74 inc. VAT)